PERSONA NON GRATA

Edited and compiled by Isabelle Kenyon

Artwork and design by Lone Buck Design

First published 2018 by Fly on the Wall Poetry Press

Published in the UK by
Fly on the Wall Poetry Press

56 High Lea Rd
New Mills
Derbyshire
SK22 3DP

www.flyonthewallpoetry.co.uk

ISBN: 978-1-9995986-1-7

Copyright © 2018

The right of the individual poets to be identified as the authors of their work has been asserted in accordance with the Copyright, Designs and Patents Act 1988. The right of Isabelle Kenyon to be identified as the editor of this work has been asserted in accordance with the Copyright, Designs and Patents Act 1988.

All rights reserved. No part of this publication may be reproduced, stored in or introduced into a retrieval system, or transmitted in any form, or by any means (electronic, mechanical, photocopying, recording or otherwise) without prior written permissions of the publisher. Any person who does any unauthorised act in relation to this publication may be liable for criminal prosecution and civil claims for damages.

978-1-9995986-1-7

A CIP Catalogue record for this book is available from the British Library

Editor's Letter:

Dear Reader,

As ever, this anthology has been curated from love and the desire to make a change - to opinion, first and foremost, as well as giving a voice to those who find themselves an outsider in our society. From circumstances of poverty, war and estrangement, this anthology is packed with poetry exploring what it means to be isolated.

Shelter is a UK charity which helps millions of people every year struggling with bad housing or homelessness through advice, support and legal services. Crisis Aid UK is a charity which supports the victims of poverty, disaster, war and oppression around the world. I am honoured to be raising funds for the important work of both these organisations.

Fly on the Wall Poetry Press gives me a purpose which fulfils me and I sincerely hope that in the strength of these poets' words, you find the creative fuel to raise your voice against injustice.

Love,

Isabelle Charlotte Kenyon

x

www.flyonthewallpoetry.co.uk
isabellekenyon@hotmail.co.uk
Twitter: @fly_press
Facebook: /flyonthewallpoetry
Instagram: @flyonthewall_poetry

Other Anthologies by Fly on the Wall Poetry include:
Please Hear What I'm Not Saying for UK Charity, Mind.

CONTENTS

1. TO BE WITHOUT A HOME p.8

Bitter Charity
By Jan McCarthy

Sleight of hand
By Nigel Kent

STRIPPED
By Marjon van Bruggen

People
By Liam Bates

BUS STOP WOMAN
Maureen Weldon

Sonnet for a Homeless Woman Named Beth
By Debbie Hall

Kitchen Tents
By Isabelle Kenyon

Forgotten hero
By Marg Roberts

Limousine Baby
By Patrick Williamson

D
By Patrick Williamson

Listening
By Ricky Ray

Derelict
By David Mark Williams

Tommy
By Kathleen Swann

2. ASYLUM SEEKERS p.27

Refugee
By Carrie Danaher Hoyt

The Refugees
By Jennie E Owen

Passing Through
By Adrian McRobb

Displacement
By Richard Archer

3. WAR/COLLATERAL DAMAGE p33

Numbers
By Isabelle Kenyon

It began with water
By Shirley Luke

Shoes
By Frank McMahon

Holocaust
By Debbie Walsh

Sostenuto
By Judith Kingston

4. FAMILY/GRIEF/THE PEOPLE WE LEAVE BEHIND p40

While your husband is still able to stand
By Deirdre Fagan

Breathing
By Debbie Walsh

Back when we were raw
By Sarah Evans

No lipstick on his collar
By Michelle Diaz

Keep Movin'
By Raine Geoghegan

Foreign
By Cathy Whittaker

Home was where my heart was formed
By Melissa Jennings

Too much blue
By Paul Beech

Birthday Trio
By Haley Jenkins

Classic Example
By Rose Drew

The roof's not free
By Rose Drew

5. INVISIBILITY p53

The Banquet
By Wilda Morris

Watching the M4 from a Maths lesson
By Olivia Tuck

Forgotten
By Marg Roberts

I envy you skeleton
By Sara Siddiqui Chansarkar

Spinner
By Scarlett Ward

In between the cracks
By Sarah L Dixon

A befriender
By Jacqueline Pemberton

Nearly Midnight
By Sujana Upadhyay

Called to Fall
By David Mark Williams

6. A MATTER OF POLITICS p65

Posted on the quiet
By Bethany Rivers

Separation
By Miriam Calleja

The day the rains came
By Adrian McRobb

Pride (Tearing down walls)
By India Kiely

The Prison Visit
By Jennie E Owen

I pledge allegiance
By Leila Tualla

Citizen of a morphing nation
By Sara Siddiqui Chansarkar

Every man we've ever hated
By Marissa Glover

7. BRITISH HUMOUR OR OPTIMISM p75

Nothing wrong with the weather
By Thomas Higgins

Tourista
By Allan Lake

Thank God for British Values
By Isabelle Kenyon

At least we tried
By Rosalind Weaver

Let's Celebrate
By Ceinwen Haydon

SECTION ONE:

TO BE WITHOUT A HOME

Bitter Charity
By Jan McCarthy

He's come look, no don't look -
I just wanted to check -
come from his den in the foxgloves
under the tumbledown bridge where cowards fear to tread
he's there he's there across across the street
bare hand in bin with gilded coat-of-arms
noblesse oblige for rubbish
lion rampant regardant,
coatless under cruel April snow -
Where is the coat we left him?

The watching curtains twitch
those who sat cosy, chicken dinners on laps
watching the Real News far far far away safe distance
suffering, you are too too close
just outside and close enough to smell
but windows are tight shut, all doors tight locked
against you, the cold, the air that makes one think

What if he's still there when we go shopping?
they say to each other as gravyed lips go twitch
they should have rat's whiskers - so should we all

He grins a rictus as he pulls it out
styrofoam box, toxic apricot nest
for probably overly-sumptuous
chicken dinner we put there before
I'll not watch now, give privacy to public deprivation

We'll get it in the neck tomorrow, we,
from the neighbours, Mr. and Mrs. Rat
they can say what they like - we deserve all kinds of guilt
and it should be about him, not about us
ladle it on: the flavour is far from alien
but bitterer now, sticking in the throat
for some hot reason I had best decipher
for my own personal, lasting, true salvation
but I fear I know: it all comes back to self
We're such cowards! We should have taken his meal to the bridge;
invited him in to eat; set a dangerous precedent
Who knows what might come of that? Eh? Think!
Rape? Robbery? Murder? An eviction order?
Ah, well in that case, friend, leave it alone.

The important thing is the roof over our heads.

Sleight of hand
By Nigel Kent

He stands over me.

I cannot see his face
only the granite grey slacks,
the diamond shine
of patent shoes,
and the red, rolled banknote,
proffered casually
between two fingers
as though some cheap
cigarette.

Fifty pounds!

Street magic
that turns a troubled
night in doorways to
a hostel day
and the luxury of
a locked door...

...but for the scratch of a match...

and the magician's hand,
transformed,
teases the surface of the note
with an obdurate flame,
browning and blackening
fledgling hopes which

stall
    and
        crash
in a spiral of
smoke and ash.

He stands over me
I see his face -
surveying the wreckage
from the height
of privilege,
before he takes off

and soars.

STRIPPED
By Marjon van Bruggen

In doorways, under bridges
in tolerant railway stations,
littered in public parks
pale slug bodies gleam through
slits in a once new suit.

I stop at one and stare.

His stained hands move aimless
through thick air, like flippers.
The underwater fire of his eyes
ship gone down with lanterns lit
keeps me prisoner.

Did he once love and live
had a wife and kids, maybe
a too small suit, neatly pressed
preserved for that special occasion?

Who took it all, and took even
more in dark silence, until
he had nothing left but this?

My dropped coins clank
so inadequate, I saunter off
hoping it is not salt.

People
By Liam Bates

Liz looks older
than she really is
'cause the wind and
close proximity
of death have
wrinkled her skin.
Kids come through
brand new to this
and Liz tries to
pass on some
hard-won wisdom.
Y'see, the
ground's colder
than the air is.
Get yourself
a set spot.
Girls are harder to
prey on in pairs.

a clean pillow
and sheets –
a proper bed.

Jess sez half
of everything
she swallows gets
fed to the baby
in her belly
so Freddie's born
premature and
methadone-
dependent.

Sal has a
nasty abscess
on her backside,
but the pain
fades dim
after the day's
first hit.

*privacy,
front door keys,
a space to just
exist.*

With a solid pitch
in front of the Co-op,
Otto sings Latvian
folk songs till some
drunks give him
a good kicking and
his broken ribs don't
ever heal right.

At night,
Rain feels safer
in the graveyard
among the dead,
till her namesake
caves in her tent,
soaks her stuff,
clouds her head.

*the relative shelter
of a squat,
at the very least.*

Trev puts ten sugars
in his tea and
scrapes together
enough cash for
bread and cheese
spread,
plus an
energy drink, 'cause
he really could use
some energy.

*they serve hot food
in the hospitals.
they serve hot food
in the prisons.*

Rob's got no
fixed address
since he left
care and these
landlords won't
accept dogs or
DSS.

just one chance,
honestly,
you won't regret it.

Ana's awoken by
articulated lorries
rolling past with
Coca-Cola snow
on their sides.
Strings of light
go up and
temperatures
drop.

Mol's had
pneumonia
twice already
and she hopes
she'll just die
this third time.

a better place.
any place
that ain't this.

Tilly's not
a prostitute,
but they
just
won't
listen.

Thank you.
Have a good evening.

Originally published in Liam's debut
chapbook, 'microwave nouveau'

Bus Stop Woman
By Maureen Weldon

There she was
late evening Bus Stop Woman.
And I waiting, with two friends,
just waiting.

"Hello."
"Hello" I say.
"I speak seven languages," she says.
"Oh ... I speak a little Irish."
"F... off, f... off," she says,
"You're mocking me." " Mocking me."

Then, she was telling me,
"I am sixty today,
I live rough,
I go to Mass on Sundays
walk these streets
for six more days..." Until...

Now her arms were around me,
I knew she was loving me
pure as her love can be.
Her grey-blue eyes and mine.
Desperate half Irish eyes.

Originally Published by Poetry Scotland and included in Weldon's collection 'Breakfast At Kilumney', published by Poetry Monthly Press, 2008.

Sonnet for a Homeless Woman Named Beth
By Debbie Hall

Her hands speak in tongues, flutter in the air,
promenade across her chest and spotlight
the words written with a Sharpie on her
shirt: ***B is for beauty/B is for Beth.***
Her long white hair waterfalls out of a
Padres ball cap as she tips it and blows
kisses to each passerby who smiles at her.
Beth's neighborhood of small tents and blue tarps
lines 16th Street just south of Petco Park.
A ribbon of chain link and razor wire
keeps the freeway at bay, forms a laundry
rack. On the corner, a shuttered market.
Tacked to a telephone pole, a sign:
Will pay cash for diabetes test kits.

Kitchen Tents
By Isabelle Kenyon

Tin cans on a bridge
ledge -
intruder
walked through your
kitchen
uninvited
(where do you heat up
your soup?)

Life's lottery:
my body designed
labelled
'HANDLE WITH
CARE: FRAGILE',
special treatment,
yours built to survive,
thicker skin.

Originally published in author's debut chapbook, This is not a Spectacle.

Forgotten hero
By Marg Roberts

Passengers on the 67 bustle past him.
Last off, the man steps down to the pavement in front of Boots
its windows sparkling with tinsel trees.

He hobbles
his mouth as dry as cotton wool.
He stretches out his arms towards the lights
red and green, as shoppers surge across Warwick Street
leaving him on the corner
dazzled.

The star-strung door to HSBC is shut to him.
He stumbles outside the gold awning of Chinese cures
gazes at Santa's sledge
bedecked with books and candles in Waterstones' cavern.

He swerves, (remembers the scrum)
unseen
round the holly-wreathed, smokers' tables outside Starbucks
under the halogen glisten, the glitz of baubles
in the Royal Priors.

Out of breath he leans on the balustrade
of the ice-cream wagon.
He licks his lips
in anticipation of raspberry dip
fumbles in pocket holes for lost coins.

Down the escalator he moves
down to longed-for iced mince pies
piled on Drucker's bar.
He stares beyond the crib and Santa's grove
in Hammell's display
to the darkness beyond

On Regent Street he searches his wallet
finds only black and white photos
dredges his memory for people he can't recall.

Limousine Baby
By Patrick Williamson

fingers the light on plate glass
as I walk past the shadows flicker
smile at me baby smile posed
in there on Andringa Straat
in the darkened hall who's there
that's me baby that's me I'm all yours
lead me up the winding stairs
do your best I'm so tight
yeh hold me baby strip me
and she stripped talking
mama laid on the bed, then
she took some coke baby did
now she's stoked up so high
her eyes are pinballs she said
this way you don't feel nothing
she said and she stroked some
two-cent perfume on her thigh this way
you don't smell nothing she said
you're hidden in the dark watch
up high she said it's a lover's
empty kiss and she stuck the vein
of death she said you don't feel nothing
with this kind of lovin'.

D
By Patrick Williamson

Drunk, swig wine
spread life on a rag
jumble in dank underpasses
upstairs flat bricked

Drunk, break chunks off
wind chill crumples self
gutted, was substance
loveless crowds hurl at you

Scream back, you cannot
think that far

Listening
By Ricky Ray

A man, tired after a day's journey,
comes to a cabin in the woods and opens the door.

The hinges squeak.
Wings shuffle overhead.

He walks in, waits for his eyes to grow into the darkness,
to make out its forms. He finds a stool by a table and sits to rest,
not wanting to try his back on the floor.
He has no sleeping bag and doesn't feel like piling leaves.

He puts his head
to the table and listens.

It speaks through his skin, his skull, his mind, tells him
all he can remember of tables—of wood, trees, seeds and growth,
of splinters, termites, rotting and soil. Eventually his mind
takes him to the edge of the field where he grows quiet and humble,
where his inner voice no longer speaks for the table, and feeling takes over.

He sits there a long time,
until his forehead begins to hurt.

Then he lifts his arm and runs his hand along the edge of the table,
slowing to finger its nicks, its rough spots, stopping at the rounded corner.
There, in the oily smoothness that might be the inner elbow
of someone he once caressed in the night,
he grasps the part of the table, the part of the tree,

the part of himself that, then as now,
he does not and cannot know.

In that shadow of time, he belongs to the cabin and falls asleep,
waking when his neck grows hot under the morning sun.

If he dreamt,
he doesn't remember.

He listens, not to the table this time, but to the living day—
the things he can hear, and the things he can't. The hinges squeak.
His stomach grumbles. A box of crackers, quiet as a skeleton,
stales in a hidden alcove behind the cupboard.

A small-breasted birdsong
slips under the door.

Originally published in author's collection
Fealty (Eyewear, 2018)

Derelict
By David Mark Williams

Wrecked car, our home sweet home,
haven to wait out the muslin rain,
windows blown out, pearls of glass
swept under scrub grass, scouring rushes.
Wrecked car turned autumn with rust
and the air stroked with falling leaves -
the only show there is, the only one for us
until the cold comes blowing breath,
and we wake to a new order of illusion.
Wrecked car, hive for feral children
who won't be saved,
their nipped wings under torn clothes
swarming over, pressing down with all the weight
their skin and bones can muster.
Wrecked car, ridden with joy and fired to skeleton,
gifted to the wood's heart,
let the weather shape it now,
let it be grown through green,
home for the hours lost, slumped
on ripped seats nothing to do but
pass the bottle round, smoke a roll up.
There's always hell to pay, but not today
all the time blown wide for us to keep,
wrecked and derelict is where you'll reach
foundation, good cheer's all you're left with
so cup the glow of it.

Tommy
By Kathleen Swann

He passed our house several times a day
steel tipped clogs clinking on the metalled road
long slow strides carrying his thin frame at an angle
head bowed like a meditating monk.
He looked so old we felt we couldn't count his years
parched skin stretched over sharp boned cheeks
blue-black shadows under cavernous eyes.
We stood pressed to the wall as he passed
not daring to breathe or speak
in case he turned his head to look at us,
the pungent smell shadowing him
wrinkled our noses but we stood stock-still
we knew he slept in a corrugated barn
with his cow and dog for warmth.
Some days he drove the cow up the road,
often he carried a bale of hay on his back
his bony shoulders and legs wrapped
in rough sacking tied with baler twine.
They said he kept money under the straw
he marked the seasons through our childhood
I can't remember when we stopped noticing him.

Originally published in a group anthology,
Write on the Farm in 2015 by Harestones Press

SECTION TWO:

ASYLUM SEEKERS

Refugee: one who has been forced to leave their country in order to escape war, persecution, or natural disaster

By Carrie Danaher Hoyt

Displaced, they wander on TV screens
With their worldly possessions in tow
Families in rags and suffering
losses and horrors untold.

Their stories of human misery
are fit into segments for news
we watch over suppers or cups of tea
in the comfort of living rooms.

When I kiss my kids and we say our prayers,
that God might grant them reprieve,
I ask myself: would I go there?
Trade my comforts for their needs?

Uncertain that I've such a measure of grace
or would sacrifice like this,
I pray God grants each one a place,
grants me selflessness more like His.

The Refugees
By Jennie E. Owen

The flood water rises steadily
and out they come. Sleeking grim
confused creatures from the tide, from the mire.
Eyes flicker copper wire, up at the black beach,
reflect the bottle of the seaside streetlights.

A flash of scale. Of ivory. Feather and fur
In flight. Closer they come. As much strangers
to freedom as they are to the peeking
audience; for fingers are twitching at the curtains now.

These refugees are unaware in their hoof and claw otherness,
that they have not left their obliterated cages,
their sunken ark,
for good, just yet.

Closer.

For the watchers are waiting now, steady handed,
all their ducks in a row.
The big game hunters, the children with spud
guns. Their mothers calling them out, hauling
rocks eye to hand at increasing speed.

Closer they come in biblical procession. Up the narrow streets,
past the cobbled stones, the chippie, pubs and churches. Past
shop fronts selling rock and candy floss in bloated bags.

Some take a darker route, the back roads and byways;
the sewers and sulphurous factories.

Closer.

When the bloody dawn breaks,
the mystery slackens, pop-pop-pop.
The invaders are too faded,
too exhausted, heavy-limbed from fighting the sea.
Eyes roll, pop-pop-pop.
Tongues loll, pop-pop-pop.
They fall, don't surrender pop-pop-pop.

They cheer hollow and howl and clap

one another on the back.
Beat their chests in slow motion over the mud bogged,
water logged, sagging
shag skinned mess of parts.

It was us or them. Was it?
It was them or us.

Whilst somewhere distant, a lone pale tiger,
the black and white kick of tomorrow's news,
purrs in a basement and licks its rusty paws.

Previously published by Here Comes Everyone 2017

Passing Through
By Adrian McRobb

Passing through...
Bundles of rags
Bin bags, itinerant luggage
Parcels tied with string
Not for posting
Broken baskets
Neglected nests
Huddled blankets
Sleeplessly shabby
Torn sleeping bags
Broken zips, a gap-toothed smile

Underpass and harassment

"Move along!"
Ignored by commuters
"Go home Abdul!"
On drunken weekends
The Chav's shout
Smug on benefits

A statistic
On a Police computer
'Refer Immigration Service'
19 PONFA* removed

Later...
In the park
20 questions
Some...unlucky
RCO (ed)*
Moved along

Through Libya
Through Italy
Through Spain
Through France

Passing through...

*PONFA=Persons of no fixed abode

*RCO=Returned to country of origin

Displacement
By Richard Archer

I came here from that land that what was once
called a cradle but is now a mass grave.
I came here from the land of unforgiving sun
where bullets buzz like hungry flies.
To leave I sold everything I owned until
all I had left was my dignity, then I sold that.
I walked here until my shoes became
scraps and my feet bled.
I rowed here until my hands blistered
and the boat threatened to capsize.
When I arrived I cried until my eyes were red
and my tears were all spent.
I tried to tell you my story but
it seems you were all deaf
Now I battle with all your paperwork,
your harsh language and your strange food.
I try to avoid the cold weather by
hiding away in my damp flat.
I work long hard hours smiling
all the time until my face hurts.
Then when I get back to my flat I cry again
until my eyes are red and my tears are spent.
Whether it's because I'm happy or sad,
I just don't know anymore.

SECTION THREE:

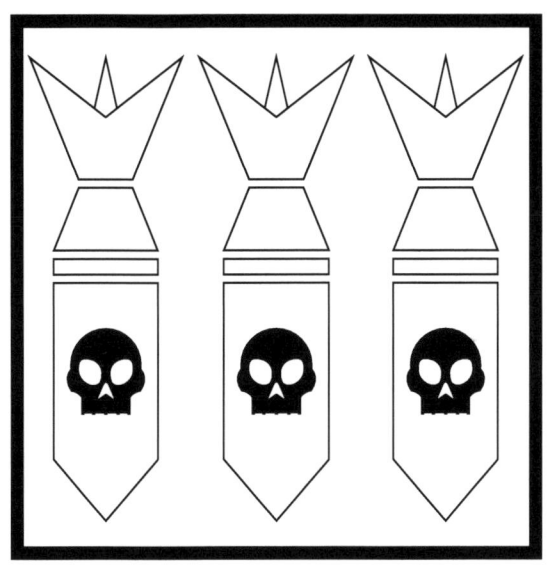

WAR COLLATERAL DAMAGE

Numbers
By Isabelle Kenyon

One million, too few for TV - cholera will die a death
so don't fuel it with firey words.
2200 dead, too few for radio -
If they were white would we have heard about it?
22 million, too many to make a difference, no point
giving it air time - tuck it under the bed.
18 million starving, think
about Yemen over your afternoon tea, just for a second,
then reward yourself a cake for your piety.

It Began With Water
By Shirley Luke

It began with water. It began with bodies in the water. It began with bodies in the water. It began with dead African bodies in the water.

It began with a ship. It began with a ship carrying human cargo. It began with a ship carrying Africans. It began with a ship carrying a cargo of Africans who became sick.

It began with a decision. It began with a decision by the captain. It began with a decision by a Dutch captain. It began with a decision by a Dutch captain to throw dead & dying Africans into the water.

It began with moans & screams. It began with the moans & screams of Africans. It began with the moans & screams of African women & children. It began with the moans & screams of African women & children as they witnessed their family & friends brought up on deck.

It began with a splash. It began with several splashes. It began with several splashes scattering the fish in the water. It began with several splashes scattering the fish as bodies disrupted the silent sea.

It began with water. It ended with death. Death became freedom.

Shoes
By Frank McMahon

Shoes, pointing in all directions
as if they could not decide which
way to go. Ahead the river,
wide and fast, its shore empty of
boats. And people. The shoes, fissured,
soiled, heels broken; children's clogs.

As they stood in their final sunlight:
prayers? Huddles of comfort? Piss and
shit leaking onto ancient leather.
Hurled backwards, no funeral flowers
save the smoke curling from the guns,
downwards, where the Duna receives
them, cold, reddening as it flows,
mere dross and cargo. A flask of
spirits opened, a cigarette
lit, safety catches on, the world
more Judenfrei.

                      Shoes, now again
pointing in all directions.

Originally published on I Am Not A Silent Poet

HOLOCAUST
By Debbie Walsh

       We watched them leaving my little brother and me
And we stood gazing gaping as they shifted

From parents to corn stalks in over-filled carriages
        And the train just repeated: 'God-angst God- angst.'

Michael held his teddy bear in a small gloved hand
        And held me, almost whole, gloved in the other.

            Looking into his dark eyes; innocence pooled
    Shouting softly, pouring hope into my heart.

I squeezed his hand and smiled.

    Somewhere there were tears, tragedy ploughed through this
        Half-closed platform - what would yield more than fear?

           In the distance, a train like a tamed ancient
       Beast drew breath-beating to a halt.

    I swung him upon my hip.

Limping he would fall beneath the dragon toothed
    Crush of brothers and sisters and mothers and fathers,

      and

      Safely seated on my safely seated knee, I felt the bite of his
Ice cold face warm. My fingers staccato through his hair.

    His palm sized head.

    Fear is noiseless; love is noiseless, felt like lightning
Forks gripping each before a fall. Thunder in your Soul.

    I didn't know that time was darkness and breath-ticked
Everywhere. I was smiling into Papa's face waking:

    Waking. My trousers wetted and a huge tear in the
Corner of Michael's eye. I hugged him. Nodded okay.

There was a huge departing crush.

    All I could see was an arm, a hand, a finger pointing
            A finger in the air pointing right or left. Michael stood
By my side.

RIGHT. Said the finger.
      LEFT. Said the finger.

    His glove slipped as they tore him away
Huge eyes kissing mine. Huge eyes kissing mine

Originally published in '21 Poems' published in the USA by Linda J. Langham, 2007

Sostenuto
By Judith Kingston

At the end of the war he did not look good,
I have to tell you.

People gave him the side eye on the train-
the regular train now, with seats and suits
and luggage racks.

No meat on his bones, no papers, no passport,
no stories, no tears,

everything wrung out of him, desiccated, condensed,
he had nothing but the will to live, to make it back
to where he was known.

Commuters hugged their bags and children closer,
looking at the way his skeleton peered through translucent skin, worried

they might catch his wasting, or his fleas, worried
he might want things that were theirs.

He was my father's uncle dressed in the skin of a ghost,
his wit muffled under the layers of horror, dulled
by the headstones that were never placed on
graves. Later, he would tell stories, but not now.

Whenever I saw him he wore a suit - his own, but
under his clothes lurked the bleached bones that
rattled in time with the train he was still on, which
could not take him from that place he never left.

SECTION FOUR:

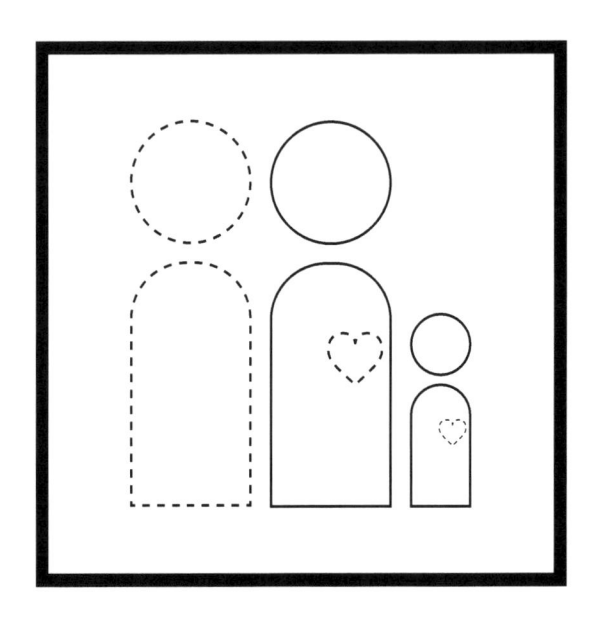

FAMILY
GRIEF
THE PEOPLE WE LEAVE BEHIND

While your husband is still able to stand
By Deirdre Fagan

you fasten the tabs
by reaching around from behind,
and your wrist is tickled by his hairy
middle, while you lean in, close your
eyes, and pause to smell the skin on his back.

when your husband tells you to call
what he's been wearing diapers
because that's what they are,
you do.

his head lowers as you finish the job.
When you get groceries, he encourages you to
take your time, enjoy being without him,
not to rush home, he is clean.

he will be fine.

no matter how many times you tell
him it doesn't matter to you,
you will be unable to unburden him.

upon learning, as you set down the groceries,
he has called an aid, instead of you,
a gift to you, the way he used to do
the vacuuming, or bring you flowers,
your own head will lower.

you will place the ice-cold coffee you have
brought him, beside his chair and thank him
for being alive.

First Published in Poetry Breakfast, 2017

Breathing
By Debbie Walsh

Breathe...

Night air barks though my trachea,
inside my lungs; it bites across my heart.

Breathe...

I stare at the fissures in my hands;
the red seas blushed within them –
my shattered nails.

Breathe...

My stomach swallows itself.
Acid surges and sinks.
Belly cramps.

Breathe...

I need a fix – you were the hand that stayed me:
your whole self a part of me, and...
you evaporated –
I tried to find mist in shadows.

Breathe...

The momentum of loss is unstoppable.
I sat caged inside, stoical –
everything fell, I was kicked away,
I rolled and rolled and ended here.

Breathe...

Loss isn't a bullet to the brain –
Loss punches inside until KO

Stop.

Back when we were raw
By Sarah Evans

We met when we were
tender winged, fresh eclosed
from the chrysalis
of childhood, balanced on
the rim of the unknown,
caught between
curiosity and fear,
pinned back by mothers
who didn't understand,
a back-of-beyond birthplace,
the bluebottle buzz of
monotony teachers and mock
of other class classmates
and nuns from a far-off planet.
We uncovered the other
in ourselves,
the joy and release
in self-disclosure,
in swigging Liebfraumilch
from the corner offy,
or lager and lime in
the Groin and Grope,
inhaling menthol fags
– peppermint is healthy –
and tongue-thrust
snogs with boys
and the beat of rock
and soul of Leonard Cohen.
Co-dreamers, we invented
Marx, feminism, CND,
in our hometown shit-hole,
where jobs depended
on building Trident.
We dreamt of flight to Uni
and finally fitting in.
Decades later we meet,
different and the same.
Our days are far
from perfect, we agree,
but the rawness settles,
wings expand and toughen,
seasoned by age.

No Lipstick on his Collar
By Michelle Diaz

The bullies can smell what he is,
even before he senses it.

Mother knows,
hides the discomfort
in a drawer full of church bulletins.

Perhaps he will become an altar boy,
take up the priesthood.

The rosary beads clack.
'*Dear God, he is not...*'

'*Mummy's boy*'.
Secrets etched onto toilet doors,
whispered down the pub.

He is made to grow up.
A couple of mix ups and a nose break later,
he finds the one.

The one is of the wrong gender.
Finds the bit that cannot come out.

Keep Movin'
By Raine Geoghegan

The last weekend in May, a Friday, we pulled up on the poove. We got the fire goin' and washed the little chavvies ready for bed. Our Ria and me were drinking mesci when our Sammy shouted. 'Dick-eye the gavvers are comin'.' All the malts came out of the vados and we stood there. We 'ad to 'old the men back as the gavvers started to wreck the site. One of 'em kicked the kittle off the yog. He shouted. 'Pack up and get going, you're not welcome 'ere.' I 'ad to 'old my Alfie back, 'e don't lose 'is temper much but when 'e does, watch out, like that time he snoped a guerro in the yock outside the beer shop an ended up in the cells for a night. It rained 'ard, we got drenched as we packed up all our covels. The chavvies were cryin', the men swearin' under their breath knowin' if they said anythin' they'd get carted off. Our Tilda was moaning about not gettin' sushi stew. Us malts started to sing,

> *'I'm a Romani Rai, a true didikai,*
> *I build all my castles beneath the blue sky.*
> *I live in a tent, I don't pay no rent*
> *an' that's why they call me a Romani Rai.'*

As the men untied the 'orses, me and Ria cleared up the rubbish. I 'eard the gavver say, 'bleedin gypos'. My Alfie called out, 'the gavvers are grunts, let's jel on, keep movin'. We kept movin' but sometimes we stayed put for a while, like when we was 'op pickin' or pea pickin'.

> *'I'm a Romani Rom, I travel the drom.*
> *I hawk all the day and I dance through the night.*
> *I'll never grow rich, I was born in a ditch*
> *and that's why they call me a Romani Rai.'*

All together in the poove
the best of times.
Thank the blessed lord.

Poove – field; Chavvies – children; Mesci - tea; Vados – wagons; Dick-eye - look there; Gavvers – policeman; Malts – women; Yog – fire; Snoped – hit; Covels – belongings; Sushi – rabbit; Didikai - half Romany & half Gorjio; Rai - a rough and ready person; Drom – road; Grunts – pigs; Jel on - let's go.

Originally published in author's pamphlet, Apple Water: Povel Panni, published by Hedgehog Poetry Press.

Foreign
By Cathy Whittaker

My husband fell in love
when she ran to him
with arms out as if he was her saviour
always wanting hug and kisses,
foreign ways.
It's not English - it's embarrassing.

The birth mother left instructions
wanted her bought up Catholic.
At least that's something.
I've taken her to Mass.
She makes me feel uncomfortable.
A foreign child in the heart of the church.

I want to send her back.

HOME WAS WHERE MY HEART WAS FORMED
By Melissa Jennings

dear mama,
when did I just become another person to you?
I know I said that I wanted us to be grown-ups, but that didn't mean I wanted us to grow apart.

when we talk on the phone, it is a radio station.
I am just one of a thousand souls that tune in.
I hear you, but I'm just a voice in your head.

you spend more time with your friends than you do with me.
I know you spent the last two decades with me, but I thought we had forever.

you tell me that other people are starting to think that you are a wife and have other kids.
I can't help but laugh;
you've never stopped caring, you just stopped being my mother.

I know you'll hate me for writing this poem, but I've found my family in words as you couldn't bring me up with my relatives: Emotional Stability and Self-Love.
I remember distinctly
you crying so many times a week when I was a child that I began to tally the amount on my skin.
I became your emotional punchbag, instead of the best thing that has ever happened.

you once told me that the happiest day of your life was when I was born, even though my father was there.
you once told me that the second happiest day of your life was when you found out that you were pregnant with me, but also that meant you had to stay with my father.
I know that I was a blessing and a curse, but it's been 23 years and I still feel like there is a womb between us.
maybe that's why I have been cruel
because I'm screaming for you to hear me over these years.

when I say "don't call me your daughter", I didn't mean go find a new one.
call me your child, the name you chose and not anyone else, but don't leave me wondering if there is something wrong with me.
my name means honeybee in ancient Greek. but, I am not a fossil to be buried.

I am not archaic. I came from you.
they say parts of our DNA are around long before we are born, roughly a century.
a part of us was born at the beginning of the 20th century, and I just want to know what year,
month, week, day,
hour, minute, and second it was
when we fell apart.

Originally published in author's collection, Underworld..

TOO MUCH BLUE
By Paul Beech

Her unborn kicks as weary she rests on a frozen bench in a bleak northern town.

Seven hours have passed since she fled his fists with naught but the babe in her womb, the clothes on her back and a small knotted bundle. Seven hours of bus after bus, caring not where she went, only to pile up the miles behind her. He mustn't find her. Must never find her.

The darkening clouds have a purple tinge, a sure sign of snow. Strangers hurry by; crows croak in a foreign tongue. Across the road, outside the Town Hall, garishly lit with coloured lights, stands a Christmas tree.

A headscarf bobs before her. A withered hand points to a door. Her unborn kicks. Then stiffly she rises, bundle in hand.

Too much blue, she thinks, crossing. Too much blue.

O for a splash of gold.

First published in the author's own collection, Twin Dakotas: poetry and prose (Cestrian Press, 2016)

Birthday Trio
By Haley Jenkins

We drank cider in a playground
under the gummiest
jungle gym we could find.

Her legs were born trying to
run to parallel horizons,
held up by supports and lies
she told about a boy who died
and left a magnum opus, a mistake baby.

He wrote poetry in gun-shapes
spoon-fed me words in new forms
belly-flopped onto thin sand,
he shook as we drew our love in ink
all over his body.

we drank cider in the rainfall
learning to fly on swings
beg for feather and bone to sprout
like waterlilies, like bindweed
out of our beaten spines.

I thought in greyscale and pixel-fuzz
built out of fat, rolls of flesh and
hungover from an old reality that echoed
and shook with the new.

he got his dickie out and I couldn't look.
we took turns kissing, tasting of sand
and sushi, that she brought up
in bubblegum cider elation,
he tore his shirt off and Darcyied
around the slides and seesaws.

And I watched and waited
for the labels I would give myself
in years to come.

Classic Example
By Rose Drew

An arcing rainbow of a wound,
pulsing purple-yellow-red,
rising to salute this failure
of choice in men,
of alcohol as mental-health management,
of careers. Does she gaze into her rum&cokes for answers,
does she startle when her spotty boss
disrupts her thoughts
of music and of angry men
and landlords banging on the door for quiet!

She has not pressed charges,
refuses orders of protection,
puts him on the phone to speak for her,
unable to explain to anyone
why she is unimportant.

She circles round the backyard with the shopping trolley,
wishing for a decent car
and knowing he will never let her have one:

He's in charge,
and shows who's boss,
and bosses her until she's just too drunk
to care
he does not care.

Folded in upon herself,
an origami girl of paper plates and paper cups,
sadness drowned with hate and shame
at fevered skin—
pulsing, purpled, welting,

unredeemed by fan or alcoholic coma
where in dreamless desperation
she fends him off forever.

From Temporary Safety by Rose Drew (Fighting Cocks Press: 2011)

The roof's not free
By Rose Drew

If you escape at night
cos your mom's insane
[beating you with sticks not cool
at 17]
Walk off to the pub,
find some friends,
end up at theirs –
but *she's* not in...

'The roof's not free' he says
sex pest
sex pest
if I don't say yes & don't NOT say no can I stay

Nothing's free
and he's bigger than me
and he covers me
and I seem to sleep,
eventually.

Dawn comes: I go.
Teddy can never know!
I'll avoid her now:
another loss that night

Hope she someday
realises
what he is like.

SECTION FIVE:

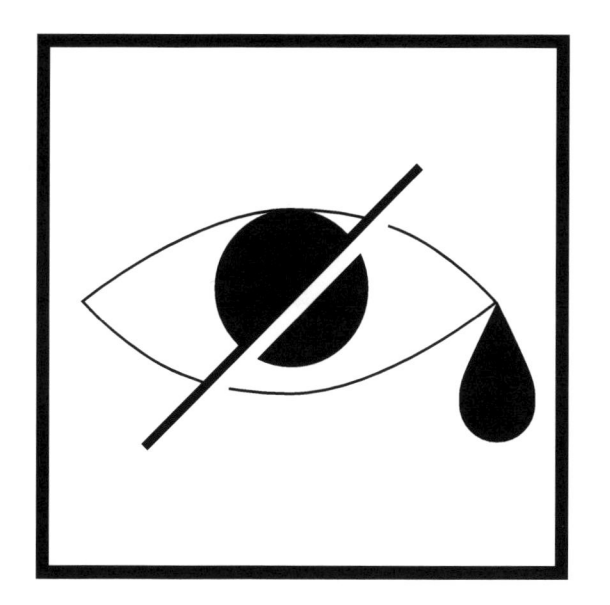

INVISIBILITY

The Banquet
By Wilda Morris

We might remember the teacher's name,
the moniker on the airline agent's nametag,

but who knows the names of those
who pick up garbage; trim trees between

sidewalk and street, sterilize toilets at O'Hare,
Heathrow or Charles de Gaulle Airport; scrub stairs,

halls and cafeterias at schools our children attend?
When we enter the gates of heaven, if there is

a hereafter somewhere beyond time and space,
the custodian will sit near the left hand

of the Almighty; the man at the shoeshine stand
who polishes dusty footwear will kneel

at the feet of his saviour and be raised up
to a place at the messianic banquet

where J. P. Morgan or Gerald Grosvenor
will polish his golden sandals; and my mother—

who spent years in a white uniform changing sheets,
cooling feverish foreheads, cleaning up vomit,

and emptying bedpans at the University Hospital,
will be an honoured guest at the head table.

Watching the M4 from a Maths Lesson
By Olivia Tuck

Each of my ribs is a logarithmic curve.
In this cold boiler room, I try being still:
my temples shiver. His voice

comes down the pipes, calling
for me to mend the heating,
and I know my brain should absorb
(the way surfaces dissolve steam).

A lot of puzzles stay puzzles.

I keep quiet - stare out into anxious sunlight,
along barbed wire axis, over scalded leaves
marking coordinates on a scatter graph.

Why are hundreds of doll's house rockets bound for Bristol?

Forgotten
By Marg Roberts

You shrank like an oyster into a shell
he cracked under his boot.

When he carried you in his arms to the cart
you thanked him, thought him kind.

Jolted inside and out, you sobbed you were sorry
-for what? His betrayal or yours? It makes no

difference. Paralysed you were useless, helpless.
Mary Ann, you cooked for him, brewed his beer

and in the good times made love to him. It made no
difference. And so he drove you like a sack of coal

to Glocester Lunatic Asylum and dumped you
while I, years later, give you words, hold you

as you take one step, slower than you wish and
still I hold you.

Mary Ann Royle (43) was admitted to Glocester Pauper Lunatic Asylum 8th September 1883 on account of 'domestic troubles.' She died there 6th July 1886.

I envy you, skeleton
By Sara Siddiqui Chansarkar

You are all bones
and bones are beautiful.
I have ugly adipose
layered on my beautiful bones.
I'm tired, dead tired
of being on the plump-cushion lists,
of caricatures of me carved on lockers,
of lonely lunches and labs,
of rarely being invited to parties,
of making floorboards quake when invited,
of sitting unnoticed with the wallpaper,
of sucking my gut in for pictures,
of being cropped off those pictures,
of sitting single in a bus seat meant for two,
of ribs being crushed in bras two sizes smaller,
of squeezing my abdomen into suffocating body shapers.
of being prescribed a meal plan by all tongues,
of gyms and their toned, snobby instructors,
of skim milks and lean cuisines,
of weighing scales and charts,
of turning off lights when making love,
of getting my body parts compared to vegetables,
of breakups without breakup-notes,
of liposuctions,
of getting my stomach stapled,
of sticking my fingers in my throat,
of tasting bile,
all the time.

Originally Published by Mojaveheart Review

Spinner
By Scarlett Ward

I am a tall tale spinner,
Braiding the fabric of myself;
Surveying my silken thread of seconds
Wound around each year of my life,
Passing it back and forth between my hands
And trying to pull some sort of sense
From out my loom of close encounters
And brief acquaintances,
Trying on their characteristics
Like an oversized second-hand coat.
With question marks for finger prints
And blank spaces underlined.
I'm still figuring out my own dimensions
To the net of this identity
And build it around myself
To see if I can fit inside
And whether I can make it feel like home.
But where is home?
Because I don't recognise myself
Outside of the cloud
Of what I have been told that I am-
Trying to find the horizon between performance
and passion,
Role, and the real me.
I am
a tall tale spinner
and that is all I can be sure of,

or it is for now, anyway.

Inbetween the cracks
By Sarah L Dixon
For Jo Bell and the 52ers

Each day she scissors the paper
into inch-wide squares,
isosceles triangles
and imperfect circles.

She won't leave the house until after dusk
and then only to source fresh paper and beige food.
She never repeats a design,
treble-checks against
her colour-coded walls.

It takes seven years
to fill the room
and another
to post each piece
through gaps in the floorboards.

She sustains splinters,
bruises and paper-cuts,
wraps fingers tight
in flesh-coloured bandages.

She imagines each scrap
butterflying its way into the space
beneath the house
settling bright
into a darkness she has never experienced.

She is motionless for a week.

Her hunger for crumpets, rusks and pasta
grumbles at the corners,
shimmies along the dado rail,
lumbers up the staircase.

There is a rainbow goat in the hallway mirror.
It has a strange red energy
and magenta eyes
that blink when she blinks.

Its indigo fur itches
where she wants to scratch.

First published in The Sky is Cracked, Half Moon Books

A Befriender
By Jacqueline Pemberton

I meet them in their sitting down years,
Moulded into high winged armchairs,
Forgotten mugs of tea
Rest on cream coloured trollies.

Meals and medication
Consume their lives,
Pendants flop on food
stained jumpers.

Sideboards are a swathe of smiling faces
They rarely see.
China cabinets stacked with tea sets
Too posh to use or part with.

Their bathrooms have grab rails,
Raised seats, non-slip mats
And in the corner
A stack of pads.

But when they talk
Their lives light up.

Ida danced on a moonlit beach
With a handsome man from Italy
She wore a red rose
In her long auburn hair.

Vinnie was a biker,
Fought the Mods at Brighton,
He could strip a bike and a woman
In the blink of an eye.

Maureen led a busy life,
Head of the typing pool at the Coop,
She kept the girls in order
And flirted with the boss.

They talk of times
When legs could race,
Hands could grasp
And flesh was bold.

The dreams they had,
The loves they lost,
The holidays they went on,
The trip they nearly took.

I fill in my next visit
On their empty calendar.

Outside the air is fresher
And my future nearer
Than I realise

Nearly Midnight
By Sujana Upadhyay

Having arrived at the party
Just as everyone was leaving
She stays on to help tidy up.
Quietly, they plod on
Clearing, wiping, sorting
The host complains about a stain
But with such mildness
She knows the party she'd been careful to miss
Had been worth it.

Elated, she feels
As if being let in on an
Inconsequential stain
Is the same as being trusted
With a long kept secret.
Elated she feels,
For proving useful
To not be expected to make small talk.
To hardly be seen.

Just before all traces of
A few happy hours are erased
She fetches her coat, giving the impression
She made herself a drink
Sometime between sweeping the floor
And emptying the bins.

From the gratitude - infused embrace
She does not immediately untangle herself.
Next time, if there is a next time,
Arrive late but bring a bottle of wine
She tells herself.

Once outside, she looks up
And waves at the curtained window
Come along? Asks a boy
With a strange voice but a friendly face
At nearly midnight.
She shakes her head,
Choosing instead the long way home,
Occasionally skipping.

Called to Fall
By David Mark Williams

They were always on the margins, quiet people
who never made much of a stir.
Nobody missed them. Their absence no more than a subtle
diminution of light in a room,
the sun going behind a white cloud,
nothing to be remarked upon.
They did not leave together, but as usual
made their way alone.
They moved like sleepwalkers,
eyes open, seeing only the line they were to follow,
as though a voice had started up in their heads,
a diode of desire tripped off, directing their steps
to where they were to go,
their designated places, their slots in the air.
They were to stand so still
that it would appear they had stopped breathing,
become stone or bronze,
gazing down on the water, the scattered flowers
of sunlight. This was how they would be captured
before they dropped out of the frame.
No shot of the fall, the splash, the last proof of them

Originally published in The Odd Sock Exchange, Cinnamon Press, 2015

SECTION SIX:

A MATTER OF POLITICS

Posted on the quiet
By Bethany Rivers

Finally, last night, I did it.
Although I'm now sitting
in a cell in this stinking jail

of sweat and fear, I'm grinning.
I stole in to the private rooms
in Westminster and I graffitied

on every wall and every mirror
the names of all the benefit suicides.
I prit-sticked photos to MPs' desks,

sellotaped them on plush seated chairs.
I then confettied the Speaking House
with photos of Aunt Beryl (put her head

in the oven), odd-job-man-Billy always
ready with a smile (took an overdose)
young Sally (mother of twins) hung herself,

stuck them down with chewing gum
along the central aisle,
all the way to the Speaker's chair.

Originally Published by I am not a silent poet

Separation
By Miriam Calleja

When I finally opened my eyes, it took me a while to adjust and stop seeing bright circles in my field of vision. My hands were stained with tar, my lips cracked. I wasn't sure if I still had a voice to use. I'd stayed there till she left. I clung to the rocks as far out as I could, until I couldn't see the orange dinghy bobbing on the horizon any more. I shouted her name for several minutes after that. Then I sat for hours hoping they would return. Had she heard me? But, more importantly, hadn't she heard that these people were just out to take her money, her passport, her identity? After some days somewhere in the Mediterranean, perhaps close to Malta or Sicily or Greece, some good person might grab her by the shoulders and escort her to safety. But that was only the best case scenario of the first part of her journey. They didn't want her there, did they? Not as much as I wanted her here. I walked back to the area where our house once stood. I chose country over love. Uncertainty was everywhere.

The day the rains came...
By Adrian Mcrobb

There had been drought
Crops were failing
Until, thank God!
It started raining

It rained until the river rose
It would surely stop?
They did suppose

In bed that night
It's rhythm settled
But, on the mountain
Nature wrestled

Earth and sand had liquefied
At first just trembled
Then started to slide
Tons of mountain
Poured right down
Invading that small
And sleeping town

Mercifully for some
Unconscious termination
But for others
Terror and isolation

Aberfan memories
That remembered dread
As Sierra Leone counts
Four hundred dead...

Pride (Tearing Down Walls)
By India Kiely

In June we leave black and white scenes
behind us and choose colour instead.
Fly our flag far above and tread
in light step with queers and drag queens.
Remember what all this pride means:
red like the bloodstains on the backs
of our hands. We all have a knack
for tearing down culture's walls.
From the first glass thrown in the brawl
turned riot, we've been under attack.

Orange like the fire she started
in my mind from the day we met.
She was wildfire, you never let
us be. She's always wholehearted
but loving girls was uncharted.
for me. Yellow like the faint lights
above hospital beds the bright
brothers of our community
died in. We came in unity
to show their blind eye wasn't right.

Green as the fields that we walked
through, twigs, branches and burrs all caught,
tangled in our hair, her laughter
like the birdsong as we talked.
Kisses for dares, I keep these locked
away, our perfect summer days.
Blue like the shimmering heat haze
the summer that Pulse stopped beating.
Things seemed improved for a fleeting
moment but their hatred still blazed

on, we are still getting killed out
here. Indigo like fireworks in
the sky, we are happy in our skin -
proudly so despite the self-doubt.
Get used to it, we've gone all-out.
Violet like the bruises we grow
shading our love til the pride goes.
Livid, vivid marks reminding
we are other. I am finding

reasons our sign is a rainbow.

This is why we march.

The Prison Visit
By Jennie E. Owen

The doors swoop down behind me and for a moment I am sealed.

Then they whir their dark magic and I am discharged.

I want to say, so polite, how nice it is.
How the concrete
leans on asphalt like poetry,
there's beauty in the metal thorns that flash
and bite. But
how could it be anything

but grey and grey.
Even sunlight
is repelled by its artificial shadow.
Thick miasma muffles
bird song,
or the memory of it,
or grass, or sky, or that ugly
crap storm that is humanity at its best.

Are you the worst?
I don't think so. Just lost,
a love letter stuck in the rim
of a post box. A pale
forgotten child.
Unwashed, unwanted.

But to me, your words sing out and I can hear them. I net them,
those peculiar birds, collect them in a jar.

I offer nothing in return.

Then,
I pass through locked doors without
a single thought
left behind. The sun
warms my face and my back
shivers.

"I pledge allegiance,"
By Leila Tualla

"I pledge allegiance,"
I begin, and a crowd of
newly minted citizens chants alongside me.
I can discern the varying accents in the people
closest to me.
We stand proud.
We stand tall facing a panel of authority,
amongst the sea of hopeful residents with hand over
their heart as they profess to denounce the
citizenship of their birth country.
Pinpricks of awareness course through me
as I lift my chin at towards a flag
I am now vowing to protect, honor, and serve.
As the applause die out,
the felicitations walk us out
of this cramped but buoyant room.
Outside, there are signs of hateful rhetoric
reminding all of us that no matter what
was celebrated, what was accomplished,
behind these closed doors
we will never be treated as equals.
We will live, love, marry, endure,
hate,
die
in a country away from our homeland;
some of us will fight and die to protect the pride of
those privilege and lucky enough just to
watch these outsiders looking in.

Citizen of a morphing nation
By Sara Siddiqui Chansarkar

The morning after the elections results night
I try to tidy up my dishevelled living room
Pick up strewn blankets and pillows
As a lone ray of sun knocks on the window

I stand and stare at the glinting suspended dust particles
The date for Naturalization looms in close proximity
Just days from reach, that elusive fruit
I had been eyeing for twelve years en route

Should I repudiate ties with the country of birth?
Knowing that my deep rooted melanin
Dark brown eyes and thick-tongued accent
Would in this milieu be met with scepticism and dissent?

Will I have to ubiquitously register myself?
Sit in surveilled booths in gatherings and stadiums?
Would yellow stars be sewn to my lapel?
A tracking band secured around my ankle?

Will my son return home from school
Whole and unbruised as he had left?
Loyalty and sentience, he'll be asked to pantomime
Else fall prey to slurs and virulent hate crimes

Will my folks traversing oceans to see me
Be tousled and paraded in airports
Before being sent on a voyage back home
For reasons unjustified and unknown

Just then, the rays of sun caress the coffee table
That houses my Naturalization Exam guide
The coffee aroma wafting in the air warms my insides
The page of Constitutional Rights reflects back the sunlight.

Originally Published in For The Sonorous

EVERY MAN WE'VE EVER HATED
By Marissa Glover

The things we've vomited will not be in the canon.

Call it art, call it protest—this persistence, this
hashtag insistence, is just us women,
scratching a name for ourselves
on history's bathroom stall to say, **We were here.**
Somewhere Philomela lost her tongue
and she's tired of being quiet.

Together, we write, we paint
with the only colors left: Rosie Red
and Pussy Pink. We plug our bruises
into amplifiers. We grab the microphone.
And we motherfucking sing.
This is not resistance. We have not enlisted.
We are not jackdaws or mockingjays.
We are nightingales, and there are bones inside
banging to get out.

Ink spills from every well, floods the stage.
At last, we've been given a single mark.
We take aim—emptying ourselves of everything.
It's easier to hold one man responsible
for these wounds than to catalogue each crime
we've witnessed, recall faces bleached from memory,
and recount all the sins still too sharp to name.

This poem was first published in Eunoia Review,
December 2017

SECTION SEVEN:

BRITISH HUMOUR OR OPTIMISM

Nothing wrong with the weather.
By Thomas Higgins

Nothing bad happening in any war,
No refugees drowning any more,
No women and children blown to bits
By bombs sold by British shits.
No rightful owners kicked off their land
By invading thieves who have planned
The deed over decades now
And now it's done, it is somehow,
As if it never happened at all
Welcome to the full masked ball.
There's nothing wrong anywhere
According to those who don't care
In the impartial media clique
Whose reporting does not reek
Of any self interest for any group
They are not just a performing troupe
Of obedient parrots trained to say
The words for which the owners pay.
No homeless problem in this land
They say they have it all in hand,
No attack on the disabled and sick
No nationwide confidence trick,
No increased numbers sleeping rough,
No rent increases making life tough
And not another reason why
There are so many lying there to walk by.
Nothing wrong with the NHS
It has not been forced to work with less,
There are no problems there at all,
It is not being set up to fall
For food banks there is no need,
These spongers use them out of greed
Zero hour contracts, only for those
Who want their freedom and who chose,
To take a job there, or to lose it all
No need to beg, just to crawl.

And there's absolutely nothing wrong
With the weather.

Tourista
By Allan Lake

There's a hard-walking tourista
at a cafe table working her phone
while having oral with a passing
cigarette. To Mum she explains
her itinerary for the week as if
everything will be the greatest
bore and chore. Palermo, Siracusa,
Toarmina. Conversation punctuated
with babytalk when her kids grab
the phone from good old economical
Grandma. Here is the kind of tourist
Sicily needs. Leaves after a week
of shopping/eating/drinking, fattening
up by partaking of the fat of the 'I land
in your backgarden on top of your
weed-choked, clapped-out economy
and poo out highly addictive euros.'
In the tradition of most invaders
she fertilises the tired Sicilian soil
for the gods of commerce then
pisses off to 'who the hell cares'.

Thank God for British Values
By Isabelle Kenyon

Taking our jobs, taking our wives,
I'm suspicious, I'm frightened,
I can't see their eyes.

I'm alarmed, I'm threatened,
by their work ethic and willing,
May's strong and stable mantra-
with their presence, they are killing.

I'm entitled, I'm ready:
let's make Britain great white
with my Anglo-Saxon, Viking, Roman, Polish blood,
I'm ready to fight.

Although we are all mongrels,
God save the Queen
for she understands what British values mean,
and generally as a country,
we're all good eggs-
for where British bombs fall, we also give aid,
and whatever the weapon, whatever the curse,
at least you can be sure, it's the taxpayer's purse!

At Least We Tried
By Rosalind Weaver

At times I come across a soul
so quick to bring me down
I wonder what their story is
and what joy they have found
in superficial conflicts
or actions brought of anger,
how do they think
that will make the world a better
place, for us to live on together?
Hearts closed to the bigger picture
this is how they respond to the suffering
of others, by increasing the fracture
till we're all just single broken bones
in a human body,
dysfunctional vessels
for a collective heart heavy.
Spreading the disease
of jumping to the worst assumptions
about another human heart
without knowing its best intentions.
But love is a doing word
so let's all keep in mind
that in a world already tough enough
at least we tried being kind.

Let's celebrate (after Mandy Coe)
By Ceinwen Haydon

Let's celebrate –
the fog clearing to admit rays
of semi-skimmed sunlight
for a few hours in mid-winter.

Let's celebrate –
my bus arriving two minutes early,
the old lady who gives
her last humbug to the driver
because he smiles like her late husband
and the Sikh boy who gives her his seat.

Let's celebrate –
my Granny's lavender oil on my wrist,
tangs of sandalwood from the old hippie
with tangled Afro hair and a pet rat up his jumper,
an albino called Ruby.
The patchouli-rich leathers of a Hell's Angel,
a fierce softie who writes poetry
to recite in the street.

Let's celebrate –
the small child who reads a book
and snuggles into his big brother,
a teenager who still sucks his thumb.

Let's celebrate –
that badass girl with purple hair,
tattoos and piercings. The one
who helps a tired mum
with her baby, heavy pushchair
and bags of Poundland shopping
to get safely off the last bus home.

Let's celebrate.

Poet Biographies

Richard Archer

Richard Archer is a poet from Walsall who writes on many subjects, tending to focus on anything that crosses his path or catches his eye. He has been writing poetry since he left school, something that continues to surprise him on a daily basis; he is also Chairman of the Walsall Poetry Society.

Liam Bates

Liam once had a poem in a little indie press's pamphlet years ago, but he can't remember the name of it. However, he does have his @wordswithpurple Instagram, which he usually can remember the name of. Also he did a chapbook; that one's called 'microwave nouveau'.

Paul Beech

Paul Beech writes poetry, flash fiction and stories for children. Published in various magazines, journals and anthologies, he enjoys reading at poetry events. His first collection, ***Twin Dakotas: poetry and prose***, came out from Cestrian Press in 2016. Paul is a retired social housing manager whose specialisms included helping the homeless. Lancashire born and bred, he now lives on Deeside, North Wales. He is a member of Chester Poets, Stanza Cross-Border Poets (Hawarden) and the British Haiku Society. Paul blogs at Grandy's Landing (http://paulbeech.wordpress.com).

Marjon van Bruggen

Marjon van Bruggen is 77 years old and lives in Mallorca, although she is Dutch. Her lifelong passion is reading and writing poetry. Over the years her work has been published in various anthologies (***Sometimes Anyway, Poetic Imagination, Better than Starbucks, Paradox***) in Literary Magazines (the NY Literary Magazine, and was shortlisted twice in a poetry contest and won an Excellence Award by them) and various others, like I Am Not A Silent Poet.

Miriam Calleja

Miriam Calleja is the bilingual author of poetry collections ***Pomegranate Heart*** (EDE Books, 2015) and ***Inside Skin*** (a two-book series in collaboration with a lith photographer, EDE Books 2016). She has also been published in poetry collections ***Please Hear What I'm Not Saying*** (2018, editor Isabelle Kenyon), and ***Poetic Potatoes*** (2018, a collaboration between Valletta 2018 and Inizjamed together with Leeuwarden 2018). Her work has been translated into Slovene in the collection ***Wara Settembru*** (2018, Slovene Writers Association). Read more on miriamcalleja.com.

Sara Siddiqui Chansarkar

Sara Siddiqui Chansarkar is an Indian American. She was born in a middle-class family in India and will forever be indebted to her parents for educating her beyond their means. She now lives in the United States. She is a Pushcart nominee for 2017 and her work has been published in The Ellipsis zine, The FormerCactus, The Same, Star82 Review, The Sidereal, and also in print anthologies. She blogs at Puny Fingers and can be reached at Twitter @PunyFingers.

Michelle Diaz

Michelle Diaz has been writing since the late 90s. She has been published in several journals, both online and print e.g Prole, Algebra of Owls, Picaroon, Atrium, among others. She was also included in the Mind Anthology *'Please Hear What I'm Not Saying'* (2018) and was recently awarded 1st prize in the Christabel Hopesmith NHS Competition judged by Wendy Cope and Lachlan Mackinnon. Her debut pamphlet *'The Dancing Boy'* is due out in 2019 with 'Against the Grain' press. Without poetry her soul would be very hungry.

Sarah L Dixon

Sarah L Dixon lived in Chorlton for 12 years. She moved in May 2017 and is currently based in Linthwaite, Huddersfield and tours as The Quiet Compere. Sarah has most recently been published in **Obsessed with Pipework, Confluence Medway, Troubadour** (Picaroon), **Please Hear What I am not Saying** and **Curlew**. She had a poem published on a beer-mat and her pamphlet, *The sky is cracked* was released by the same press in November 2017 (Half Moon). Sarah's inspiration comes from many places, including pubs and music, being by and in water and adventures with her seven-year-old, Frank. She is still attempting to write better poetry than Frank did aged 4! Frank's line, aged 4, was "Is your heart in a cage so it doesn't fly away?" http://thequietcompere.co.uk/

Rose Drew

Rose Drew is an immigrant from America. She used to feel more smug about that, 'til June 2016. Rose co-hosts monthly open mic York Spoken Word (running since January 2006), and is the editor and events manager for Stairwell Books. Her creative work, mostly poetry, has been published in anthologies, newsprint, and journals, including Connecticut River Review, Fairfield Review, Strong Verse, One Hundred Days (ed Andrea Brady), I Am Not A Silent Poet (edited by Reuben Woolley) and *The Machineries of Love* (Ragged Raven Press). Her book *Temporary Safety* (Fighting Cock Press) was No 9 on 2011 Purple Patch 20 Best Individual Collections.

Sarah Evans

Sarah Evans has had many short stories published in anthologies, magazines and online. Prizes have been awarded by, amongst others: Words and Women, Winston Fletcher Prize, Stratford Literary Festival, Glass Woman and Rubery. Other publishing outlets include: the Bridport Prize, Unthank Books, Riptide, Best New Writing and Shooter. Writing poetry is a more recent venture, with work appearing in *Please Hear What I'm Not Saying*, placed second in the 2018 RNIB competition and several other shortlistings.

Deirdre Fagan

Deirdre Fagan is a widow, wife, and mother of two who has published poetry, fiction, and non-fiction. Most recently, her work has appeared in *Amaryllis, New Verse News, Nine Muses, The Opiate, and Rat's Ass Review.* Her poem, "Outside In," was nominated for *Best of the Net 2018* by Nine Muses. Fagan is also the author to *Critical Companion to Robert Frost* and has published a number of critical essays on poetry, memoir, and teaching pedagogy. She teaches literature and writing at Ferris State University where she is also the Coordinator of Creative Writing. Meet her at deirdrefagan.com

Raine Geoghegan

Raine Geoghegan, MA, is of Romany, Welsh and Irish ancestry. Her poems and short prose have been widely published both online and in print. Her debut poetry pamphlet, *'Apple Water - Povel Panni'* will be launched in November 2018. She recently read at the Ledbury Poetry Festival alongside the film, 'Stories from the Hop Yards' in which her work was featured.

Marissa Glover

Marissa Glover teaches and writes in central Florida, where she spends most of her time sweating, swatting mosquitoes, and trying to find her place. Her poetry has appeared in UK journals such as Amaryllis, Picaroon Poetry, Solstice Sounds, Poetry24, Bonnie's Crew, Clear Poetry, I Am Not a Silent Poet, and Ink, Sweat & Tears. Follow her on Twitter @_MarissaGlover_.

Debbie Hall

Debbie Hall is a psychologist and writer whose poetry has appeared in the San Diego Poetry Annual, A Year in Ink, Serving House Journal, Sixfold, Tuck Magazine, Poetry24, Bird's Thumb, Poetry Super Highway and other journals. She has work upcoming in an AROHO anthology. Her essays have appeared on NPR (This I Believe series), in USD Magazine, and the San Diego Union Tribune. She received an honorable mention in the 2016 Steve Kowit Poetry Prize and completed her MFA at Pacific University in Forest Grove, Oregon. Debbie is the author of the poetry collection, *What Light I Have* (2018, Main Street Rag Books).

Ceinwen Haydon

Ceinwen lives in Newcastle upon Tyne, UK, and writes short stories and poetry. She has been published in web magazines and in print anthologies. She graduated with an MA in Creative Writing from Newcastle University in 2017. She believes everyone's voice counts. @CeinwenHaydon https://www.facebook.com/ceinwen.haydon

Thomas Higgins

Thomas Higgins is sixty four years of age and began writing poetry at the age of fifty six. He lives in the West of Cumbria in NW England. He has been awarded a gold award for a poem submitted to the NY Literary Magazine, which was published in the June 2016 issue. Thomas is listed on Reverbnation as 4th nationally for spoken word, and 38th globally.

Carrie Danaher Hoyt

Carrie Danaher Hoyt is a lifelong lover & writer of poetry. She lives in Massachusetts where she is a wife and mother of three school-aged kids; in addition, she works as an estate planning attorney. You can find Carrie's poetry in The Cabinet of Heed, Amethyst Review, The Pangolin Review, Twitterization Nation, and thegreenlightjournal.com. She also has poems forthcoming in Anti-Heroin Chic and 8 Poems Journal. Carrie is on Twitter @CDanaherH.

Haley Jenkins

Haley Jenkins holds a Creative Writing Master's Degree from The University of Surrey and a Creative Writing Bachelor's Degree from The University of Roehampton. In 2016, Haley was awarded First Prize in the Elmbridge Literary Competition for her short story 'Talisman' and in 2014 won 3rd Prize in the Hopkins Poetry Prize. She has been published in two anthologies by Fincham Press - *The Trouble with Parallel Universes* (2014) and *Screams & Silences* (2015), as well as publications such as, Rag Queen Periodical, Guttural Magazine, Tears in the Fence, painted spoken and The Journal of British & Irish Innovative Poetry. Her work has also appeared in online zines such as datableedzine, epizootics and ez.Pzine (Pyre Publishing). Haley's first poetry chapbook was published by Veer Books (August 2017). She also runs Selcouth Station Press.

Melissa Jennings

Melissa Jennings (they/them) is a trans non-binary indie author who lives with their cat, Dora, in the sometimes sunny but always vibrant city of Glasgow, in Scotland. They are currently studying towards an MA in English Literature at the University of Glasgow. Melissa has published three poetry collections, *Afterlife*, *Dear Judas*, and *The Body Remembers*. Their second full-length poetry collection, *Underworld*, will be released on October 10th 2018.

Shirley Jones-Luke

Shirley Jones-Luke is a poet and a writer of color. Ms. Luke lives in Boston, Massachusetts U.S.A. She has an MA in English from UMass Boston and an MFA in Creative Writing from Emerson College. Shirley was a quarter finalist in Nimrod International's poetry contest and Adelaide Magazine's poetry contest. Shirley participated in the Split This Rock Poetry Festival in April of 2018. She has been published in Water: Black Bodies. Adanna Journal, Deluge, Longleaf Review and For the Sonorous. Shirley was a Summer 2018 participant at Breadloaf, Tin House and VONA workshops.

Nigel Kent

Nigel is a reader and writer of poetry living in Worcestershire. His poetry has been shortlisted and longlisted for several national competitions and has been published by South Magazine, Dempsey and Windle, Paper Swan Press, Hedgehog Poetry Press, Emma's Attic Publishing and the PSOU. It has also been translated and published in literary magazines in Romania.

Isabelle Kenyon

Isabelle Kenyon is the editor of Fly on the Wall Poetry Press and the author of chapbooks, *Digging Holes To Another Continent* (Clare Songbirds Publishing House, New York) and *This is not a Spectacle*. She has a Jackrussle called Rocky. Social Media: @kenyon_isabelle (Twitter); Fly on the Wall Poetry (Facebook) and @flyonthewall_poetry (Instagram). www.flyonthewallpoetry for editing enquiries, book reviews, poetry shop and updates!

India Kiely

India Kiely is a young author, poet and blogger currently studying Creative Writing. Her work can be found on Instagram and Twitter (@sapphicauthor) and discusses issues of womanhood, bisexual identity and mental health among other things. If she's not buried in a journal, you can find her cuddling her dog or in search of a great book to read.

Judith Kingston

Judith Kingston is a Dutch writer living in the UK. Her poetry has been published on Poets Reading the News, performed in a number of Off West End immersive theatre productions and her pamphlet *'Signs and Wonders'* was recently shortlisted for publication by Against the Grain Poetry Press. A teacher by day, Judith likes to put her whiteboard pens to good use after office hours leaving her poetry on mirrors, windows and tiled floors. Follow her #stealthpoetry on Instagram: @judith_kingston and Twitter: @judithkingsto

Allan Lake

Originally from Saskatchewan, Allan Lake has lived in Vancouver, Cape Breton Island, Ibiza/Spain and Tasmania. He now calls Melbourne home and visits Sicily often.
He has published two collections; *Tasmanian Tiger Breaks Silence* (1988); *Sand in the Sole* (2014) plus the chapbook, *Grandparents: Portraits of Strain* (1994). Lake won Elwood (Aus) Poetry Prize 2015 & 2016, Lost Tower Publications(UK) Poetry Comp 2017 and Melbourne Spoken Word Poetry Festival/The Dan Competition 2018.

Jan McCarthy

Jan McCarthy writes novels, short stories and poetry, and has been published in several anthologies and e-zines. Her books include a series of seven *'Rainbow Tales'* written for her grandchildren. Her articles on bipolar self-management have appeared in the magazine of Bipolar UK. She leads Birmingham writing group Fun With A Pen and is a member of MIND and Writers' HQ.

Frank McMahon

Frank has been published online in I am not a Silent Poet, The Poet by Day, Riggwelter, The Cannon's Mouth and Cirencester Scene. He has poems soon to be published in The Curlew. McMahon also writes plays and one will be broadcast in October on Corinium Radio.

Frank also writes short stories and is working on a children's novel. He has another play to appear soon on Soundworks.

Adrian McRobb

Adrian McRobb was born in 1955 and was brought up in West London. He now resides in the North East of England in Cramlington. His poetry has appeared in literary magazines including, First Time, The Linnets Wings and in several poetry anthologies. Since 2014, he has had many poems published by his local paper, the most notable of which, Flying North, about the Flying Scotsman. In 2017 one of his poems was selected to appear on a banner, displayed in Sandersons Shopping arcade Morpeth. Adrian regularly performs his work at poetry recitals and open mic events. He won first prize in the Morpeth Gathering Literary Competition in 2013, and is a past holder of the Lowford Trophy. This year 2018 Adrian broke a local event record…he came First, Second, Third, and Fourth in the Open English Verse Competition. This has never been done before, since the competition started in 1968. He runs a local poetry group with co-hosts Mandy Maxwell and Hannah Welfare.

Wilda Morris

Wilda Morris is the Workshop Chairperson for Poets & Patrons, and former president of the Illinois State Poetry Society. She is widely published in journals and anthologies. Her book, ***Szechwan shrimp and fortune cookies: poems from a Chinese restaurant***, was published by RWG Press. Her blog at wildamorris.blogspot.com posts a contest for other poets each month.

Jennie E. Owen

Jennie E. Owen's writing has won competitions and has been widely published online, in literary journals and anthologies. She is a Lecturer of Creative Writing and lives in Mawdesley, Lancashire with her husband and three children.

Jacqueline Pemberton

Jacqueline was born in Ipswich, Suffolk but has lived in the North West for over twenty years. She is an active member of writing groups in Southport, Wigan and Preston. She retired from teaching four years ago because of ill health and now enjoys her work as a volunteer for the Reader charity sharing poetry with older people who have dementia. She has three grown up children and three young granddaughters who she loves very much.

Ricky Ray

Ricky Ray was born in Florida and educated at Columbia University. He is the author of *Fealty* (Eyewear, 2018) and the founding editor of Rascal: a Journal of Ecology, Literature and Art. His recent work can be found in The American Scholar, The Matador Review, Amaryllis, Scintilla and One. His awards include the Cormac McCarthy Prize, the Ron McFarland Poetry Prize, the Fortnight Poetry Prize, and a Whisper River Poetry Prize. He lives in Harlem with his wife, three cats and a Labradetter. Their bed, like any good home of the heart, is frequently overcrowded. Visit rickyray.co and rascaljournal.com for more.

Bethany Rivers

Bethany Rivers' pamphlet, *'Off the wall'*, was published by Indigo Dreams (2016). Previous publications include: Envoi, Cinnamon Press, Obsessed with Pipework, Three Drops from a Cauldron, The Ofi Press, Picaroon, Bare Fiction, The Lake, Tears in the fence, The Lampeter Review. She mentors the writing of memoir, novels and poetry: www.writingyourvoice.org.uk

Marg Roberts

Marg Roberts was Warwick's poet laureate in 2009-10. Some of her poems have been published online: Algebra of Owls, and Ink Sweat and Tears. Some in magazines: Reach and Orbis. Marg used to work in the probation service and tends to write poems about individuals who don't quite fit in. Her novel, *A Time for Peace* was published by Cinnamon Press in October 2016 and and is set during WW1 in Serbia- whose story is often neglected.

Kathleen Swann

Kathleen Swann is retired from a career in the NHS. She has lived in Cumbria and North Yorkshire and enjoys reading and writing with poetry groups in both of these places. Her work has been published on-line for 'I'm not a Silent Poet' and on poetry websites. She has been in print in *Poetry Scotland, This Place I Know, Write on the Farm, Pieces of Cake* and will be included in the next edition of Speakeasy 3 Magazine. Kathleen is preparing a collection of her work to be published next year

Leila Tualla

Leila Tualla is a Filipino-American memoirist, poet, and Christian author. Leila's books include a YA Christian contemporary romance called, Love, Defined and a memoir/poetry collection called *'Storm of Hope: God, Preeclampsia, Depression and me.'* Her poetry is featured in a few mental health anthologies, *'Please Hear what I'm not Saying'* and *'We are Not Alone: Stories of Mental Health Awareness'*. She is currently working on a chapbook series of identities; the first one, 'not your token,' is out and explores Asian stereotypes and growing up brown in small town America. Leila lives in Houston, Texas with her husband and two miracle babies.

Olivia Tuck

Olivia Tuck has had pieces published in literary journals and webzines including The Interpreter's House, Lighthouse, Amaryllis (where she was nominated for the Forward Prize for Best Single Poem) and Three Drops from a Cauldron. Her work also featured in *Please Hear What I'm Not Saying*, the Fly on the Wall Poetry charity anthology on mental health. Olivia starts at Bath Spa University this autumn, to study for a BA in Creative Writing. She's always been an outsider, but writing has definitely helped! Find her on Twitter: @livtuckwrites

Sujana Upadhyay

A keen observer, Sujana Upadhyay carries around many stories and anecdotes in her mind, and can often be found telling a few out loud to no one in particular. She considers herself a storyteller, and theatre and poetry are her chosen medium. She was mainly raised in Nepal and currently lives in the UK. Her work, including short stories, essays, reviews and poems, have been published widely both in the UK and Nepal.

Debbie Walsh

Debbie Walsh studied at Edge Hill University and was awarded MA with distinction and the Rhiannon Evans Poetry Scholarship in 2011. Her poetry sequence *Nimbus Movements* is published by Knife Forks and Spoons Press.

Scarlett Ward

Scarlett Ward is a 25 year old snail mama, witchcraft enthusiast, and poet working from Staffordshire, UK. Her poetry event at Caffe Del Nino was short listed by Saboteur Awards for best spoken word event, and her work has recently featured in anthologies from Verve Press, Nothing Books, and Fishbowl Publishing.

Roz Weaver

Roz is a poet and spoken word performer from the North of England who began writing in 2017 and performing in 2018. She has been published in Catalogue of Failure, Dear Damsels, Whisper and the Roar, Morality Park, Yellow Arrow Journal, Persephone's Daughters, as well as the poetry anthologies 'Further Within Darkness and Light' and 'Essential Existentialism - The Meaning of Life'. This year, her work was displayed at the annual Rape Crisis Conference and as part of 'Testimony', a London multimedia exhibition held at the international NoVo Foundation Conference, as well as her work being displayed and performed at the 'The Sunlight Project' London exhibition.

Maureen Weldon

Maureen Weldon has published five chapbooks, the most recent being Midnight Robin 2014 published by Poetry Space Ltd. Summer 2017 Second Light Live, she won Poem of the Month, for her poem Midnight Robin. 2014 she represented Wales at Ukraine's International Poetry Festival, Terra Poetica, where her poems have been translated and published in Ukraine's International Journal Vsesvit. Maureen is very widely published, recent publications, Crannog magazine, Spring Issue 2018. Poetry Scotland magazine, and Poetry Scotland Open Mouse. Ink Sweat & Tears. *Lifejacket Liverpool*, an anthology edited by Lew Kelly.

Cathy Whittaker

Cathy has a sequence of 15 poems published in *Quintet*, Cinnamon Press. Her poems have appeared in Under the Radar, Prole, The Interpreters House, Envoi, Orbis, Ink Sweat and Tears, Southlight, Obsessed with Pipework, The Magnolia Review, Mslexia, and other magazines. She was shortlisted for the Bridport Prize, won the Southport Writers Competition and was placed second in The Welshpool Poetry Competition. She was published in *#Me Too A Women's Poetry Anthology* edited by Debra Alma.

David Mark Williams

David Mark Williams lives in southwest Scotland. He is widely published in magazines and anthologies. His poems have won prizes in several competitions. He has been shortlisted for the Montreal Poetry Prize, won Second Prize in the New Zealand Poetry Society International Competition and short listed for the Aesthetica Creative Writing Award. This year he won the inaugural Hedgehog Press Slim Volume of One's Own Competition. His first full length collection of poetry, *The Odd Sock Exchange*, was published by Cinnamon Press in 2015. His second Collection, *Papaya Fantasia*, will be published by Hedgehog Press in November 2018. Some of his poem performances have been made into short films by photographer, Kim Ayres, and are available to view on You Tube.

Patrick Williamson

Patrick Williamson lives near Paris. He is a poet and translator and has published a dozen works. Recent poems in I am not a silent poet, And Other Poems, Blue Nib Press, Paris LitUp, International Times, and Mediterranean Poetry. Next collection (due shortly) is Traversi (English-Italian, Samuele Editore), and, previously, note Gifted (Corrupt Press), and Locked in, or out? (The Red Ceilings Press). He is the editor and translator of The Parley Tree, An Anthology of Poets from French-speaking Africa and the Arab World (Arc Publications). Founding member of transnational literary agency Linguafranca.

About Fly on the Wall Poetry Press

Fly on the Wall begun with anthology, 'Please Hear What I'm Not Saying' for UK mental health charity, Mind. Since then, it has evolved into publishing charitable anthologies, quarterly online magazines and will soon be publishing individual author collections.

Fly on the Wall Poetry is edited and run by Isabelle Kenyon. Please do feel free to get in touch via email at isabellekenyon@hotmail.co.uk or by subscribing to the website and blog www.flyonthewallpoetry.co.uk